SOAR!
Study Guide

BUILD YOUR VISION FROM THE GROUND UP

T. D. Jakes

Faith Words

New York   Nashville

FaithWords
Hachette Book Group
1290 Avenue of the Americas, New York, NY 10104
faithwords.com
twitter.com/faithwords

First Edition: November 2017

FaithWords is a division of Hachette Book Group, Inc. The FaithWords name and logo are trademarks of Hachette Book Group, Inc.

The publisher is not responsible for websites (or their content) that are not owned by the publisher.

The Hachette Speakers Bureau provides a wide range of authors for speaking events. To find out more, go to www.hachettespeakersbureau.com or call (866) 376-6591.

Scriptures are from the *Holy Bible*, New Living Translation, copyright © 1996. Used by permission of Tyndale House Publishers, Inc., Wheaton, Illinois 60189. All rights reserved.

ISBN: 978-1-4555-5392-1

Printed in the United States of America

LSC-C

10 9 8 7 6 5 4 3 2 1

Contents

CONTENTS

Introduction

I'm thrilled that you're choosing to utilize this study guide to enhance your engagement with my book *SOAR!*. This guide is designed to help you think through all that is required for you to build your vision and launch the dream you've been carrying inside you. Whether you want to start a new business, create a nonprofit, organize a new agency, or launch a new ministry, the following questions and exercises will equip and empower you as you elevate your understanding and application of *SOAR!* to even greater heights.

This guide is designed to help you personalize the material as much as possible, so how you use it is ultimately up to you. You can work through it as you read *SOAR!* to maximize your experience, use it to stimulate thoughtful discussion with others in a small group or book club, utilize it as a central resource from which to build your vision, or all of the above! The format here follows each chapter of the book with clear, easy-to-understand questions and complementary material. You only need to read the Introduction in the book to start your engines and prepare for takeoff.

I've deliberately created both the book and this guide to apply to a wide spectrum of new ventures and creative endeavors. Therefore, even if you're planning to discuss the material with others, going through it first by yourself, taking as much time as you want, may be the most productive way to benefit and grow from the interactive exercises that follow. I strongly encourage you to take the questions seriously and to be as specific and personal as possible in your responses.

After you've absorbed and integrated the material to your satisfaction, you will find sharing your ideas with others in a group setting to be a great way to maximize the material's impact. Because your responses will be uniquely personal, please remember to respect the dreams of others by showing them the same courtesy and kindness you want to receive. A community of kindred entrepreneurial spirits provides a wonderful laboratory for you to help others' visions be realized. Try not to discourage or criticize one another, and certainly you won't want your discussion to degenerate into gossip or inflammatory judgment of any kind.

Completing this guide can lay the runway for your vision to take flight as smoothly as possible. No matter how you choose to use it, I pray that this process will cultivate new ideas and inspire you to take greater risks in pursuit of bringing your dreams to life. The best is yet to come, my friend, so get your pen ready and prepare to *SOAR!*

SOAR!

Study Guide

CHAPTER 1

⬦

Ignite Your Flight

Putting Dreams in Motion

Often, the beginning of a journey may be propelled by the sheer thrill of embarking on a new adventure and by the adrenaline-laced excitement of new discoveries. Before you take a long trip, the planning and preparation may be as enjoyable as the actual voyage to your destination. You get to imagine what the journey will be like and enjoy the luxury of endless possibilities, including a smooth departure and gentle landing.

If you are reading my book *SOAR!* and have now decided to supplement your encounter with the material by completing this study guide, then you have likely already spent a great deal of time dreaming about the vision inside you. Maybe you've imagined quitting your job and launching your own business, finally enjoying the freedom, flexibility, and financial autonomy you've been craving. Perhaps you've envisioned reprioritizing your life so you can finally focus on fulfilling your God-given purpose instead of the expectations of those around you. You might even have day-dreamed about what it would take to invest your time, energy, and efforts into an endeavor uniquely yours.

Well, now is the time, my friend, to ignite this process and move forward with doing what you and you alone were uniquely created to do on this earth. Right now you are taking the first step in a life-changing journey toward ultimate success. Let's get started!

1)   Do you remember the first time you flew in a plane? What were the circumstances? How did you feel as you left the ground and flew across the sky? What did you like about the experience of flying for the first time? What scared you or caused you concern? How do your answers to these questions apply to the process of getting your dreams off the ground?

_____

_____

_____

_____

_____

2)   What comes to mind when you see or hear the word *entrepreneur*? Do you already consider yourself an entrepreneur? Why or why not? What do you have in common with entrepreneurial pioneers such as the Wright brothers? What do you think you're lacking that most entrepreneurs seem to have?

_____

_____

_____

_____

_____

Our parents, both directly and indirectly, are usually our earliest and most profound teachers. Both by what they say and perhaps more importantly by what they do, we learn what it means to mature into responsible, capable, successful individuals. I suspect some of the greatest lessons we learn from our families involve work and our attitudes toward our talents, gifts, and abilities. We absorb information and impressions about what it means to earn a living, how to spend and save money, and how to maximize our earning potential.

Depending on our family's structure and functionality, we might have learned some lessons that inhibited our growth and limited our ability to realize the gifts God gave us. For example, many women inherited the remnants of rigid gender roles that dictated a dutiful life of domesticity. While it's a wonderful calling to be a stay-at-home mother and homemaker, and it's certainly a full-time job in itself, this role should never imprison women and prevent them from exploring their full career potential. In order to move forward with building our vision, we must learn what we can from the lessons of our family while shaking off limitations and liabilities that would inhibit us.

3)   What did you learn about the nature of work from your family growing up? Were there entrepreneurs hustling in your household? What positive traits did they model that became part of your work ethic?

_____

_____

_____

_____

_____

4)   What criteria do you use when you consider someone successful in their career? Annual income? Net worth? Possessions and status symbols? Work ethic? Personal

fulfillment? Popularity? Service to the community? Something else? Using your criteria, how successful do you consider your parents or the family members who raised you?

_____

_____

_____

_____

5)   As you look back, what barriers prevented your parents and family members from being more successful? Were these barriers more external (circumstances, illness, etc.) or internal (lack of confidence, personal insecurities, etc.)?

_____

_____

_____

_____

In our formative years, we often see ourselves based on the way others see us and the messages they tell us about ourselves. In addition to the legacy of our parents, most of us have been shaped by our social, cultural, economic, and geographical environments as well. Our work ethic, self-confidence, and willingness to take risks may have been influenced by peers, teachers, pastors, and mentors in both positive and negative ways.

Consequently, we may have cultivated certain perspectives on what it means to be an entrepreneur, and a successful one, within our communities.

As you begin the process of bringing your vision to life, you may benefit from some soul-searching to determine your understanding of an entrepreneurial mind-set along with any self-imposed barriers that have been holding you back. Some of these may seem obvious, while others may require you to reflect on your past experiences and relationships. While I'm not saying you need therapy to clear your mental runway, it can be helpful to discuss your thoughts, associations, and feelings with a trusted individual who can listen and encourage you to realize the latent greatness within you. Knowing what is motivating your vision can go a long way toward sustaining it and following through with the actions required to launch it.

6)   What has kept you stalled on the runway in your pursuit of advancing both personal and professional endeavors? What have you overcome to get to where you are now? What barriers do you currently face in bringing your vision of success to life?

_____

_____

_____

_____

7)   What motivates you to want more in your life—financially, emotionally, personally, professionally, relationally—than you have presently? Is it more money? Self-autonomy from being your own boss? More freedom and control in your life? More personal fulfillment? More alignment between your values and your lifestyle? Something else?

_____

_____

_____

_____

8) What specifically compelled you to pick up *SOAR!* and begin considering how to apply it to your life at the current juncture where you find yourself?

_____

_____

_____

_____

_____

_____

Financial incentive is often a powerful motivator as we consider the reasons fueling our desire to build and launch a new business or other enterprise. While there's nothing wrong with wanting to make more money and enjoy the fruits of our labor, I urge you to be cautiously optimistic about the financial realities ahead of you during the process of building and launching your vision. Most entrepreneurs, innovators, artists, and inventors experience a season of sacrifice and financial struggle as they ramp up and get their vision off the ground. Having realistic expectations about your profit margins and the time required to have them in hand is a crucial part of a healthy entrepreneurial mind-set.

We must also guard our hearts against greed and the idolatrous love of money. In the Bible we're told, "For the love of money is a root of all kinds of evil. Some people, eager for money, have wandered from the faith and pierced themselves with many griefs" (1 Tim. 6:10, NIV). You'll notice here that it's not money that's the problem—it's our love for it *above all else.* Your desire for financial success is but one ingredient in the mixture of motivators fueling your success. It must be tempered by your passion for whatever field, industry, cause, or product you hope to bring to the rest of the world. In addition, it helps if you have a passion for adventure, for discovery, for new people and places if you want to keep a balanced perspective and to reach new heights.

9) Do you agree that the desire to make more money is, by itself, insufficient to fuel your ultimate pursuit of success? Why?

_____

_____

_____

_____

10) What are some ways having more money in your life would improve it? What are some ways having more money would complicate your life right now? What can you do to keep a healthy, biblical attitude toward money?

_____

_____

_____

_____

Economic realities influence and sometimes determine our options and actions almost every day. They determine where we go, what we do, how much we spend on a cup of coffee, and where we call home. During the economic downturn of past years, abrupt changes in finances meant that some people lost their jobs, their cars, their houses, and even their entire retirement savings. They were forced to downsize in ways they could never have imagined as well as to put the pursuit of all dreams on hold.

These harsh realities may have appeared so limiting and prohibitive that it was hard to imagine ever having the resources and funding required to build and launch your vision. But as our country's citizens have rebounded, many have discovered a resilience and resourcefulness within themselves that they didn't know existed. In fact, many people with an entrepreneurial mind-set respect their economic limitations without allowing these realities to block their forward progress. They believe in the old saying "Where there's a will, there's a way" and channel their frustrations into a fierce determination to soar higher than ever before.

11) How have economic conditions of the past few years affected you and your family? What changes or sacrifices have been made in order to sustain your standard of living?

_____

_____

_____

_____

12) How can current economic and social conditions work in your favor as you begin moving forward to actualize your dreams? What challenges do they present? How do you feel as you consider launching a new venture in the current cultural climate?

_____

_____

_____

_____

Faith is an integral ingredient for an entrepreneurial mind-set. Whether we look within the pages of the Bible or reflect on past personal blessings, we see that God is the ultimate entrepreneur and opens doors that no human could have opened. Because we are created in his image, we are given an incredible responsibility and opportunity, one that's inherently part of how we're made. We have been given a piece of our Creator's limitless and powerful creativity.

God imbued each of us with both intellect and imagination, with an analytical side to our brains joined to a creative side. While he could have created any and every object we use every day, he instead equipped and empowered us to create them with the raw materials he provided. For instance, God gave us trees because he knew that trees could provide us with wood, which could then be cut, crafted, and carved into innumerable tools, building materials, and decorative objects. Building and launching your vision is about taking the materials God has given you and aligning them with the physical essence of the dream he's placed inside you.

13) Do you agree that God is the "ultimate entrepreneur"? What favorite Bible stories or familiar passages come to mind when you consider his vast creativity, transcendent ingenuity, and supernatural resources? Considering that you are created in God's image, what can you learn from his example?

_____

_____

_____

_____

_____

14) How are you using the resources God has placed in your life and dropped in your lap? Make a list of all resources that you have within reach to support and to assist you in building your vision from the ground up. In addition to funding from your personal accounts and those of investors, don't forget to include intangible resources such as

relationships, your reputation, and local resources, such as inexpensive office space or a growing local economy, on your list.

_____

_____

_____

_____

_____

CHAPTER 2

Winds and Trends

Know Your Conditions

Knowing the environmental conditions into which you will build and launch your vision is essential for your success. In fact, you must consider winds and trends even before you design your business and attempt to get it off the ground. Knowing the environment where your business will operate provides you with the necessary data to help you make decisions about your design, your delivery, and your destination.

While technology and modern science allow us to control and alter so many aspects of life that our ancestors could never have dreamed possible, the weather remains unpredictable and mostly uncontrollable. Storms still blow up without warning, and the sun can pierce through clouds transforming it into a picture-perfect day.

When traveling, you can ignore the weather along your route only at your own peril. Instead you must look at the direction of the wind, the cloud cover, the temperature, and the storm fronts to help guide your journey. Similarly, you must look at the context and cultural conditions of the venture you want to create and launch. These environmental factors enable you to make the best, most informed decisions possible as you craft a plan to build and launch your vision.

1)   When was the last time you found yourself unprepared for bad weather—caught in a thunderstorm without an umbrella, driving on icy roads without snow tires, or enduring scorching temps without sunglasses and sunscreen? What prevented you from preparing for the possibility of such harsh conditions? What will you do differently the next time you visit a similar location during the same time of year?

_____

_____

_____

_____

2)   Why is it so important to consider winds and trends before you begin building your vision? How does understanding current market conditions allow you to make better choices about the way you design your new business, nonprofit, or ministry?

_____

_____

_____

_____

In his comparisons and parables, Jesus often used weather conditions to symbolize the trials we face in life. One of my favorites from the Bible seems especially apt as we consider winds and trends:

Everyone then who hears these words of mine and does them will be like a wise man who built his house on the rock. And the rain fell, and the floods came, and the winds blew and beat on that house, but it did not fall, because it had been founded on the rock. And everyone who hears these words of mine and does not do them will be like a foolish man who built his house on the sand. And the rain fell, and the floods came, and the winds blew and beat against that house, and it fell, and great was the fall of it.

Matthew 7:24–27, NIV

Obviously, you want to build and launch your vision on solid ground with a firm foundation of faith. Anyone can call themself an entrepreneur and purchase a domain name to sell something online, but only the true visionaries willing to work hard and singularly focus their efforts can soar to the greatest heights. Only entrepreneurial thinkers who have anticipated and prepared for change can maximize their success.

Your new venture must weather all kinds of conditions, some you know about already and others you can only discover once you're in the air. That's why you must keep your finger raised to gauge the force and direction of the winds around you. That's why you must be prepared for changes in the temperature and weather patterns of your cultural climate. Winds and trends can sink the *Titanic*, but they can also be harnessed to empower your ability to take flight and soar!

3)   On a scale from 1 to 10, with 1 being the most unfavorable and 10 being absolutely perfect, rate the following "weather conditions" for building and launching your new venture:

- ☐ Local economy
- ☐ Local workforce
- ☐ Latest indicators within your industry, field, or area
- ☐ Your competition
- ☐ Public perception of your product, service, or venture
- ☐ Production costs
- ☐ Operating costs
- ☐ Start-up costs
- ☐ Your reputation or perceived brand identity

☐ Scalability—your ability to expand, grow, and/or franchise

☐ Other factors unique to your venture (list them here):

Recently, before starting my TV talk show, I tested the climate and discovered I would be flying against the wind based on changes and current conditions. This awareness resulted in building my team with experienced partners who helped me succeed despite the many challenges we faced.

4)   As you consider the impact of all weather conditions related to building your vision, are you flying against the wind or with the wind at your back? How will this influence the design of your new venture?

_____

_____

_____

_____

_____

The other way to explore your environment for clues on how to design your business plan is to look at what needs fixing, changing, or solving. This method looks from the *outside in* and isolates problems or conditions currently affecting the social and cultural climate around us. You may notice the need for a new product or invention to help people handle lifestyle changes due to technology, the economy, or migration patterns. You may see an opportunity that appeals to certain demographics or regional interests.

Similarly, you may see the spark of a new trend and fan it into a full-blown wildfire. It sees something good and knows it can be made better, perhaps through exposure and promotion to a wider audience. It's the reason we see so many copycat products and businesses follow in the wake of a major success. If a certain genre of TV show or movie explodes, then you can be certain that similar ones will follow. Sometimes the weather changes to your advantage without any attempt on your part to influence it. You may not even know what caused the wind to shift until after the storm has hit!

5)   What item, product, or service would make your life easier right now? Which one is most needed in your local community right now? What opportunity do you see based on current conditions in your airspace?

_____

_____

_____

_____

6)   What's required for you to provide this needed commodity to those around you? How economically feasible is it to launch and provide these goods? In other words, how can you make a profit providing this to potential customers?

_____

_____

_____

_____

Time and time again, prospective entrepreneurs tell me they aren't "creative" enough to come up with an original idea, invention, or innovation. And I always say, "No problem—just take something people want or need in your area and do it better than anyone else!" You don't have to reinvent the wheel—you just have to make it go smoother and faster.

Scripture tells us there's "nothing new under the sun" (Ecc. 1:9, KJV), and this holds true for your new venture as well. Basic humans needs—food and drink, shelter, clothing—continue to sustain millions of enterprises in the form of restaurants, hotels, and boutiques, just to name a few. Many products and services that we use the most and care the most about allow us to become experts without even realizing it.

7) What products or services might you consider yourself an expert on? Do you drive across town for the perfect cup of coffee? Know just where to find the best little black dress? Know just who to call when you need a caterer for your office party?

_____

_____

_____

_____

_____

8) Once you've identified a few of these products and services on which you've become an expert, think about what you would do differently if you were the owner of such a business. In other words, what's lacking that you could use to attract customers and distinguish your venture from the competition?

_____

_____

_____

_____

9)   Make a list of the possible products, goods, or services on your short list for launching a new venture. Which one do you know the most about already? Which one do you feel most passionately about? Which one do you think would sell most easily in today's conditions?

_____

_____

_____

_____

_____

_____

10) What are the physical parameters of the area you want to service with your goods or services? Why have you chosen this area?

_____

_____

_____

_____

_____

11) Who are your primary customers and how much do you already know about them? Once you narrow your target customer base, you would be wise to find out as much about them as possible: average age, marital status, and average size of household, whether they rent or own their home, their ethnicity, average income, level of

education, and number of hours typically spent working each week. Do you know this information about your current target audience? How can you obtain such vital information about them?

_____

_____

_____

_____

_____

12) If you launched this new venture, who would you be competing against? What would you be doing differently than your competition to distinguish yourself from them?

_____

_____

_____

_____

_____

When I was starting out in both ministry and entrepreneurial business ventures, I suspect I felt similar to pioneers like the Wright brothers. Just as they had a primary destination in mind, I needed to build something to get me from point A to point B.

Consequently, I added staff members, expanded facilities, and employed experts in technology, along with the various support systems needed to sustain them all.

With more than 300 employees now, I have built a vision that serves both my ministry and my entrepreneurial endeavors. My staff includes people skilled in graphic design, shipping and receiving, catering, music and film production, and a variety of other areas I never imagined needing to support my work. In order to fulfill the potential that God gave me and make the most of the opportunities he presented, I had to invent something uniquely mine.

Now it's time for you to do the same thing. You must consider the distance between where you are and where you want to go. Then you can design, build, and launch your vision to reach the divinely appointed destination that is yours and no one else's. You will need help along the way, but it all starts with you. No matter how high you plan to fly, you can't start it, maintain it, and take it higher if you aren't involved in its original construction!

13) Under the best of conditions, what would your new venture look like at its most successful? How large would it need to grow to get to this peak? What can you do now as you design it that will enable it to grow to fulfill its potential?

_____

_____

_____

_____

_____

14) What entrepreneur, company, or organization best serves as a model for the kind of venture you would like to launch? How much more research do you need to conduct

in order to learn about your model's path to success? How can your role model inspire the design as you bring your vision to life?

_____

_____

_____

_____

CHAPTER 3

✦

Damsel, Arise!

When the Wind Is Blowing Your Way

While I understand and appreciate having various translations of the Bible available, I often return to the one I grew up hearing in church, the King James Version. Often hearing or reading the KJV forces us to slow down and carefully consider the words before us. Such is the case with the passage that inspired my title for this chapter as it reveals an incident in which Jesus healed the daughter of a synagogue leader named Jairus (Mark 5:35, KJV).

Slowed by the crowds surrounding him, and healing the woman with the issue of blood along the way (Mark 5:25–34), Jesus arrived at Jairus's house and was told it was too late—the man's daughter had died. Apparently a crowd had gathered, some to see what Jesus would do, I suspect, with others there to mourn and help the family. That's when Jesus showed up and basically asked everyone, "What's all this commotion about? This girl is not dead, only sleeping." Sure enough, the Lord then stood over the bed where this young lady was lying and told her to wake up.

> And when he was come in, he saith unto them, Why make ye this ado, and weep? the damsel is not dead, but sleepeth. And they laughed him to scorn. But

when he had put them all out, he taketh the father and the mother of the damsel, and them that were with him, and entereth in where the damsel was lying.

And he took the damsel by the hand, and said unto her, *Talitha cumi*; which is, being interpreted, Damsel, I say unto thee, arise.

Mark 5:39–42, KJV

I thought of this story because I believe God wants you to wake up and breathe new life into old dreams that others—and maybe even you—thought died long ago. But as we see in this poignant scene, with faith in God's power, all things are possible. It's not too late—there's a vision inside you that's about to come to life!

1) Do you believe God has anointed this next season of your life for you to build and launch your vision? How has he prepared you and equipped you so that you can bring your dreams to life right now?

_____

_____

_____

_____

_____

2) What does it look like for you to "arise" from your sleepy past and embrace your new, wide-awake future? What needs to change in your perspective—on God, on life, on work—as you enter into this new season?

_____

_____

_____

A recent study by the Economic Policy Institute (EPI) found what most people, especially those over forty, already know: very few are financially prepared for retirement (ww.epi.org/publication/retirement-in-america/#charts). During the economic downturn of the past decade, many lost most or all of their retirement savings and investments. Compounding the problem, many employers cut benefits, which, along with the rising cost of living, forced people to drain their 401(k), IRA, and savings accounts. The EPI study discovered that the average working-age family has only about $5,000 saved, and often their savings account also serves as an emergency fund (http://www.cnbc.com/2017/04/07/how-much-the-average-family-has-saved-for -retirement-at-every-age.html).

If this news alarms you, you're not alone, because millions of people are unprepared to take care of the old woman or old man they will one day become. The good news, however, is that it's not too late to add new streams of income, revenue that can create a new infrastructure upon which to build your retirement. If you're willing to plan ahead, just as my mother did with her many rental properties, then the hard work you invest in now can yield a harvest in years to come.

3) What preparations have you made for your "golden years" or for the time when you no longer work at your present vocation? How would launching your vision for a new venture affect your life ten years from now? Twenty years? Thirty years?

---

4) What's one simple step you can take today to take care of your future older self, just as my mother did? How would taking this step right now benefit you in the long run?

_____

_____

_____

_____

_____

_____

As I've shared many times, I was blessed to grow up with parents who modeled an extraordinary work ethic. My mother in particular faced social and cultural barriers in her day that impeded and even prevented many women from exercising their gifts and abilities. Nonetheless, some women found ways to break into career fields traditionally populated by men. They also practiced a resourceful resilience that stretched their family's budgets and allowed them to bring in more income by working part-time, selling cosmetics, catering meals, or whatever they could find to make extra money.

While many glass ceilings have been shattered by talented and tenacious women, others remain. Women still do not earn as much as their male counterparts in most corporate businesses and industries. They continue to fight sexism and harassment in the office. But they also continue to thrive, finding creative ways to get ahead just as their mothers and grandmothers did. Whether we're male or female, we can learn from these strong women who model an irrepressible and indomitable entrepreneurial spirit!

5) Who were the strong women in your life who influenced your work ethic while you were growing up? What did you most admire about them and the choices they made? Why?

_____

_____

_____

_____

_____

6) What qualities and traits do you share with these strong female role models in your life? How can their examples empower you to break through the social, cultural, and economic barriers that have been holding you back?

_____

_____

_____

_____

_____

It's always easier to look for excuses than opportunities, but if you want to build your vision and soar, then it's time to extinguish your excuses once and for all. If you want to get started and take action to realize your dreams, then you must begin where you are. Whether you realize it or not, God has already blessed you with an abundance of resources and equipped you with custom-made abilities from your many personal and professional experiences. You must start where you are with what you have, just like Moses did.

> Moses answered, "What if they do not believe me or listen to me and say, 'The Lord did not appear to you'?"
> Then the Lord said to him, "What is that in your hand?"
> "A staff," he replied.
> The Lord said, "Throw it on the ground."
> Moses threw it on the ground and it became a snake, and he ran from it. Then the Lord said to him, "Reach out your hand and take it by the tail." So Moses reached out and took hold of the snake and it turned back into a staff in his hand.
>
> Exod. 4:1–4

7)   What do you have in your hand right now, like Moses with his staff, that the Lord can use to help you start your new venture? What abilities, skills, talents, and experiences do you currently possess that can be harnessed toward getting your vision off the ground?

_____

_____

_____

_____

_____

8) What excuses have you made already or conditions have you set to prevent you from building your vision? What's required for you to move forward without having perfect conditions or everything you think you need?

_____

_____

_____

_____

_____

9) What does it mean for you to "start small" so you can "finish big"? What's one action step you can take this week toward starting small?

_____

_____

_____

_____

_____

One of the most frequent excuses I hear from would-be entrepreneurs is that they lack the financial resources to bring their vision to life. And I continue to tell them what I'm telling you: money helps but is never the fundamental fuel for your new venture. In order to succeed, you don't have to have wealthy investors or an enthusiastic panel from *Shark Tank* to launch your venture.

Now more than ever you can great start new ventures with fewer resources than previous dreamers. Online tools and social media allow you to minimize costs while reaching a global audience of potential constituents. These opportunities level the runway for getting big dreams and small businesses off the ground. If you're willing to be creative, resourceful, and innovative with what you already have, then you'll be surprised what you can build and how well it can fly.

10) Do you agree there's never been a better time to build and launch your new venture? Why or why not? What risks are you most concerned about as you move forward?

_____

_____

_____

_____

_____

11) How can technology be harnessed to facilitate taking small steps forward as you bring your dreams to life? In what areas of development have you underutilized technology? What assistance or resources do you need in order to maximize the benefits and advantages of the internet, social media, and smart- phone technology?

_____

_____

_____

_____

_____

Making money is a worthy goal for your new venture. As the primary motivation for what you want to build, however, it will serve you poorly. Any ideas of experiencing overnight success and getting rich quick floating around must be grounded by more realistic expectations. If you're only building and launching your vision to make a lot of money fast, then you will most likely be disappointed—and broke! Being an entrepreneur is a mind-set, not a money set. If you don't passionately love the process involved in your new venture, your fiscal infatuation will quickly fade as practical matters remove the romantic veneer.

Having an entrepreneurial attitude means being a problem solver, not just a money-maker. It's good to want to succeed and make a profit, but it's even better if you know why you're doing it—and what you'll do with success once you achieve it. Knowing your entrepreneurial motivation can fuel a strong, elastic, and flexible sense of determination that can overcome any obstacle and make the most of every opportunity.

12) What are your greatest entrepreneurial strengths? How can these be focused and channeled toward building and launching your vision successfully?

_____

_____

_____

_____

13) What weaknesses and areas of inadequacy within yourself do you need to address in order to prevent them from impeding your momentum? How can you compensate for these soft spots to ensure that you remain patient throughout the process of launching your vision?

_____

_____

_____

_____

_____

14) If you had all the money you needed to live comfortably for the rest of your life, would you still want to build and launch your vision? Why or why not?

_____

_____

_____

_____

CHAPTER 4

It Takes Two

Inspiration & Innovation

Whether it's *Star Trek* or *Star Wars*, Aretha or Beyoncé, *Good Housekeeping* or the *Real Housewives*, almost everyone growing up in our country has been influenced, both directly and indirectly, by a multitude of media. TV shows, movies, music, magazines, books, even commercials and ads all bombard us with messages about ourselves, our families, our appearance, and our work. Many times we may not realize the messages we're absorbing, but because we're surrounded by them, it's important to think through what we've picked up and whether these messages are actually true.

Just think about how long it's taken to see balanced diversity reflected in television programs and movies. When you only see people similar to yourself in certain, often stereotypical, roles in the shows you watch, it can be difficult for you and for others to let yourself soar. But keep in mind that just because you haven't seen others similar to yourself doing what you want to do, it doesn't mean it can't be done. Every generation has its pioneers and trailblazers, individuals with an entrepreneurial spirit willing to abandon socially prescribed roles and to create their own unique path. You are one of a kind and so is your vision—don't be afraid to go where others have not yet gone!

1)   What were some of your favorite TV shows and movies when you were growing up? Which characters were role models for you in some way as you moved into adulthood? How did certain characters and actors influence your career choices in some way?

_____

_____

_____

_____

_____

2)   Who were the other cultural and historical pioneers who spoke to you during your formative years? What was it about them that attracted you? Why?

_____

_____

_____

_____

_____

Stories offer us powerful insights by providing metaphors to help us see our lives and situations differently. For this reason, Jesus often relied on parables throughout his ministry, teaching his listeners by basing his stories on characters, places, and incidents familiar to them. His parables provide a symbolic, objective vantage point from which to consider issues of humanity, forgiveness, grace, and love.

Stories can also help us see beyond our own experiences and consider other people's perspectives, especially if they're critical of us. For example, when confronting King David over his infidelity with Bathsheba, the prophet Nathan chose an indirect route and told the king a story that helped objectify the crimes David had committed (2 Samuel 12). David was incredibly moved by Nathan's story and outraged over the injustice described in the story. Then, of course, David realized that he himself had perpetrated such an injustice by stealing another man's wife and manipulating circumstances to kill the man.

I chose the myth of Daedalus not only because of its unique connection to flying but also because of the way it symbolizes the resourceful ingenuity latent within all of us. So often we feel trapped by circumstances, with no options to help us maneuver toward our long-term goals. We always have choices, however, and can take small steps no matter how busy, overwhelmed, and demanding our schedules may be.

3) Can you relate to the myth of Daedelus crafting wings to fly out of the labyrinth? What other myth, parable, story, or Bible personality best expresses your feelings about the barriers you face in trying to get your venture off the ground?

_____

_____

_____

_____

_____

4) What obligations, responsibilities, and demands currently form your personal labyrinth? How have they limited your ability to move forward with building your vision? How can you rise above them to pursue your vision?

_____

_____

_____

_____

_____

_____

Inspiration is a funny thing and can spark inside you during the most mundane moments. For individuals cultivating an entrepreneurial mind-set, inspiration is often like breathing, a life-giving flow that both inhales images, ideas, and interests and exhales new creations, expressions, and innovations. Like a baby maturing into a child and then an adult, your dreams are now experiencing a major growth spurt as you take action toward making them tangible and concrete.

Part of this growing process is allowing inspiration to happen naturally and trusting your imagination as a creative furnace where new, innovative solutions can be forged. The sources of your inspiration will also change as you change. Sometimes you begin with one idea and realize the real opportunity lies in something you discover accidentally. Numerous successful ventures have been launched because of something that went wrong in the process of its development. Thinking like an entrepreneur not only means thinking outside the box but above, below, and beyond the box!

5) How would you define "inspiration" as it pertains to you as an entrepreneur? Write out your definition here and then compare it with a dictionary definition. What's uniquely personal about the way you define this most important concept?

_____

_____

_____

_____

_____

6)   What events, ideas, and personalities have inspired you as you've formulated the vision you want to bring to life? What or who has been the greatest inspirational force so far? How have they energized you to move forward?

_____

_____

_____

_____

_____

Being innovative means being able to use the resources that are available to create new products, new solutions, and new procedures. Innovative people learn to see what others can't or won't envision. Innovators throw off the blinders of convention and ignore the obstacles of practicality in order to work in tandem with inspiration and, like Daedalus, look up for a way to fly from the confines of circumstance.

Innovators take a preexisting foundation and build a new house, creating a new blueprint along the way. What inspiration started and imagined in a person, innovation then improves upon. This might involve making an existing product, service, or procedure more effective, more efficient, or even just more exciting. It sometimes means finding a way to bring style to something that is merely functional, such as a chair or table. Other times, being innovative requires you to solve a problem and come up with a hybrid that combines the best of several other ingredients. Innovation allows you to take a good thing and makes it better by making it your own.

7) Similar to what you did with defining inspiration, what does "innovation" mean to you? What companies, people, and products do you consider innovative? Why?

_____

_____

_____

_____

_____

_____

8) Do you consider yourself an innovative person? How so? What innovations have you made in your life recently? How about with your work—what systems, products, or services have you helped to innovate?

_____

_____

_____

_____

_____

_____

_____

_____

You'll recall that in the myth of Daedalus and Icarus, his son, the boy ignored his father's warning and flew too close to the sun, which caused the wax that held his wings together to melt. Like a daredevil without a parachute, Icarus started freefalling through the sky and landed in the ocean. He allowed the thrill of immediate success to eclipse his perspective and objectivity.

While Icarus's failure was fatal, entrepreneurs usually discover that failing at their endeavors isn't nearly so dangerous. Instead, failure may be a powerful teacher providing you with new data about what will and will not work as you build your vision and attempt to launch it. Early failure often reveals the limitations of your vision's design and uncovers its weak spots, allowing you to reinforce and rebuild as needed. Often the best way to succeed in the long run is to learn from your own shortsightedness and errors in judgment that produce wisdom if you're willing to persevere.

9)   What has happened when you've tried to build and launch your vision in the past? What can you learn from those attempts? How can they both inspire you and help you innovate a new direction for your venture?

_____

_____

_____

_____

_____

10) Are you more afraid of failing with your new venture or experiencing immediate success with it? What challenges does each scenario offer? How can you prepare for early success so that you don't end up flying too close to the sun?

_____

_____

_____

_____

Entrepreneurs trying to get a new venture off the ground must not only be attuned to winds and trends, they must also harness the powers within themselves—their intellect and imagination. These twin engines of ingenuity allow you to customize your new creation and to learn and grow along the way. Sustaining flight won't be easy, and even after you rise above the labyrinth of wrong turns and dead ends you mustn't allow the bright sunshine of success to melt your wings. And if they do melt, then pray for a soft landing and get ready to build another set of wings!

Regardless of what attempts to limit or constrain you, I know you can rise above it all. You were made to soar, so don't allow the vertigo of victimhood to sideline you or send you plummeting to the ground too soon. God has given you a vision and the resources required to build it. Now is the time to get in sync with inspiration and innovation and discover how they can take you soaring to new heights.

11) How can you synchronize both inspiration and innovation to empower your design for this new venture?

_____

_____

_____

_____

_____

12) What will sustain you when you encounter conflicts and crashes in the start-up process? How long are you willing to keep trying in order to get your vision off the ground?

_____

_____

_____

_____

CHAPTER 5

◈

Flight Plan

Your Blueprint for Success

The importance of planning and having a blueprint for your new venture cannot be underestimated. Lack of this vital component causes many would-be entrepreneurs to fail when they don't follow through. They assume that a good idea will lead to an easy method for getting their business, nonprofit, or ministry off the ground. Then when problems arise or obstacles pop up—and they always do—visionary builders lack the foresight to solve them, and in some cases remove them, before they end their venture's flight prematurely.

Having an entrepreneurial mind-set aligns the power of planning with persistence in action. If you rely on either extreme, you will likely not get very far off the ground, if you rise at all. Planning alone accomplishes nothing, and obsessive planners can become paralyzed fr because they keep tweaking their plans, wondering if they've thought of every contingency and its solution. Similarly, going it alone is sorely limiting and will never lead you to realize your venture's full potential. Unlike the proverbial bull in a china shop, doers need focus and a plan of action that channels their energy in the right directions.

1) Do you consider yourself more of a planner or a doer? Do you usually read the instructions before trying to assemble new equipment or appliances? Or do you just start trying to put the pieces together, following your intuition and being guided by past experience?

_____

_____

_____

_____

_____

_____

2) How much time do you usually spend thinking about and planning new projects before you actually start? How well has this worked for you in the past? As you consider your new venture, what aspects need more planning?

_____

_____

_____

_____

_____

_____

The Bible counsels us that "hope deferred makes the heart sick, but a longing fulfilled is a tree of life" (Prov. 13:12, NIV). With this vibrant metaphor in mind, you don't want to plant something only to watch it wither and die before it bears fruit. You want a healthy sapling that grows into your sturdy tree of life. Or to use our metaphor of flight, you don't want your flying machine to hover over the runway—you want it to reach 30,000 feet as you speed toward success!

When you consider ultimate success as your destination, then you can work back from your future arrival there and create a flight plan to get you there. This flight plan allows you to compare all of the research and reflection you've accomplished and to design your vision accordingly. Knowing weather patterns, wind speeds, and the environment where your business will live, you can build something capable of enduring in such conditions. Focusing on solving your problem and knowing something about who you want to target, you're ready to put it all together into one document that can serve as your master plan.

3) How much of a written plan do you already have for your new venture? What has kept you from completing it in the past? Or, if you're just getting started, what do you need to begin putting it together?

_____

_____

_____

_____

_____

4) What areas of your new venture have been researched and clearly thought through? Which areas still need further research and development before your plan is complete?

_____

_____

_____

_____

_____

Many people tend to be intimidated by the process of crafting a business plan, but it doesn't have to be something formal and complicated. It simply needs to be clear, thorough, up-to-date, and cohesive. In fact, the more complicated you make it, the less useful it may turn out to be. Make your flight plan something that's practical, focused, and comprehensive in its ability to instruct, inspire, and entice you. You can always revise it, daily if necessary, and update it with your latest discoveries and revelations.

The key, however, is that you simply start and put something down on paper. If it helps, tell yourself that you're just going to brainstorm on the page for a while and see what happens! Take the pressure off and allow yourself to get organized as you think through the various stages your new venture requires.

5) What intimidates you most about putting together your business plan? How can you address these fears and concerns so that you're free to come up with the best blueprint for your venture?

_____

_____

_____

_____

_____

6) As you plan how to bring your vision to life, what are the unique aspects you need to consider related to this particular industry, field, or area?

_____

_____

_____

_____

Business plans range in size from one page to hundreds of pages, so there's no one-size-fits-all model. I recommend beginning by simply thinking through as many aspects of building and launching your vision as possible. Whether you want only a basic sketch or a more detailed big picture, or something in between, your business plan is yours and should reflect you and how you will need to use it.

The *SOAR!* Flight Plan included in this chapter is designed to help you generate the raw material you will need to craft a thoughtful, thorough business plan. There's nothing magical or formal about it, so just begin by answering the questions as specifically as possible in regard to your new venture. These questions may not all be relevant, but most of them address areas of development and execution you will at least want to consider before you actually start construction on your endeavor.

7) Have you completed answering the questions in Chapter 4 of *SOAR!* to help start your business plan? If not, take the time to finish answering each series of questions as specifically and thoroughly as possible. It may feel like a pain now, but, trust me, you'll be glad later!

_____

_____

_____

_____

8) Which sections of the *SOAR!* Flight Plan—What, Who, Why, Where, How, When—were the hardest to answer? Why? What do you need to do to think through these areas with full confidence?

_____

_____

_____

_____

A good business plan removes as many potential obstacles to your pursuit as possible and provides solutions for the inevitable problems that remain. Basically, your plan allows you to think in multiple dimensions so that you can imagine your new venture and see it from all facets, smoothing off rough edges and creating the best design to showcase your product or service.

Like an engineer building an enormous bridge across a river, you want your plan to anticipate the stress points where daily wear and tear might weaken and erode your structure. In addition to providing present solutions for future problems, your flight plan can also provide you with confidence to know that you're doing everything in your power to fly high before you ever leave the ground. Conflicts will still arise and a crisis may still threaten your venture, but you have reinforced the stress points and made sure that all the small details—and the larger areas they support—are addressed.

9) What are the greatest stress points with your current plan or blueprint? In other words, what are its limitations when current conditions change? How can you anticipate such possibilities and build them into your plan?

_____

_____

_____

10) When the unexpected happens or something goes wrong, how well can you improvise and find another direction or solution? What can you do to cultivate more dexterity as you launch your venture?

_____

_____

_____

_____

_____

As I confessed to you at the end of this chapter, I have not always followed my own advice here and drafted a business plan for every new venture I've started. Without a doubt, however, I can assure you that when I didn't write out a flight plan, I eventually suffered the consequences of flying by the seat of my pants! Without a plan, I was forced to slow down, conduct vital research that should have already been completed, brainstorm new solutions, test their viability, and then learn the hard way which ones worked and which ones didn't. Even when I haven't drafted a business plan, at some point I've always wished I had!

Nonetheless, I've learned from my mistakes and now try always to look ahead not only at what's probably going to happen next but also what other possibilities and contingencies could occur. Such mental and physical preparation, like the groundwork before I speak or preach, may go unseen or unused, but having such preparation completed gives me the freedom to ensure a smooth landing. Remember, *preparation facilitates liberation*.

Your business plan can make sure you not only take off and soar to new heights but also that you know how and when to land and take off again. You'll never fly to the fullness of your potential without first studying the sky!

11) Are you ready to show the draft of your business plan to your mentors and would-be investors? What parts of your plan still need attention?

_____

_____

_____

_____

_____

12) Set a deadline for yourself to have your business plan, at least a first draft, completed. I encourage you to be realistic, considering all your other responsibilities, but to finish it as soon as possible.

I will finish my business plan by _____.

CHAPTER 6

✦

Invisible Wings

Riding the Winds of E-Commerce

When I was growing up, shopping meant a drive to the supermarket for groceries, a trip to the local mall, or a visit to various shops and boutiques scattered around town. It took quite a bit of time in our family's schedule and, of course, took place during the business hours of the various merchants, whether those times were convenient for us or not. Certain items, like a new appliance, and certain times of the year, such as Christmas, complicated our shopping excursions even more because we knew they required even more of our precious time.

The emergence of e-commerce solved those problems of time consumption and inconvenience by allowing us to conduct business, shop, and purchase products and services any time of day or night—at our convenience, not the sellers'. Not only can I order almost anything from groceries to Gucci online, I can do it from the comfort of my home in my pajamas. E-commerce created an entirely new landscape of commercial transactions. The same phenomenon that freed you from having to shop in brick-and-mortar stores can also free you to connect to your constituents.

1)   How would you describe your attitude toward e-commerce and using technology to build and launch your vision?

_____

_____

_____

_____

2)   Are you old enough to remember a time when you didn't shop online? Or, like me, can you remember the time before the word *e-commerce* even existed?

_____

_____

_____

_____

3)   What were your first impressions of shopping online in the early days of technology? Or, if you've grown up with the internet, when you were younger?

_____

_____

_____

_____

4) Were you an early adapter who began shopping online as soon as you discovered eBay and Amazon? Or were you reluctant to make purchases online until it was proven to be a worthwhile time-saver?

_____

_____

_____

_____

_____

_____

While it may seem relatively new, e-commerce—basically the selling, buying, and transacting of business online—has become the fastest growing segment of our country's economy. In 2016, total e-commerce sales were estimated to be almost $400 billion, an increase of more than 15 percent from the previous year. Overall retail sales were up by roughly 3 percent, with e-commerce sales accounting for about 8 percent (www.census .gov/retail/mrts/www/data/pdf/ec_current.pdf, accessed May 1, 2017).

You don't have to be an accountant or economist to understand what these numbers mean. E-commerce is here to stay and has become an enormous part of any entrepreneurial equation. It opens up the world as your online shopping center and gives you the freedom to engage with constituents you might never encounter otherwise. Doing business online is not going away and will likely become more competitive over time. Many consumers and users now assume that merchants have at least a basic website or online sales portal. To ignore e-commerce is to leave yourself in midair without both engines!

5) How long did it take you to get comfortable shopping and purchasing items through the internet? What's the ratio of the physical shopping you still do compared with the online commerce you transact?

_____

_____

_____

_____

_____

_____

6)   What kinds of products and services do you currently purchase online? How fre-quently do you shop online? What sites are your favorites for browsing and "screen shopping"?

_____

_____

_____

_____

_____

_____

E-commerce must be a crucial part of any new entrepreneur's business plan, whether you plan to begin selling online or set that as a future goal of your enterprise. In fact, e-commerce is often a good way to test your product or service before launch-ing it full-scale. Such a test flight also begins the process of building relationships with your core constituents. Many people are willing to provide feedback and to offer sug-gestions if they know their input is being taken seriously. In exchange, you not only receive valuable intel about how to make your venture better before your next takeoff, but you also connect with valuable members of your target audience.

7)   How does e-commerce fit into your current business plan? Is your new venture originating online or do you envision technology and social media supplementing what you will do from your home, office, church, or storefront?

_____

_____

_____

_____

_____

8)   How can you use technology and e-commerce to build relationships with your target constituents? Will your new venture have its own website, domain name, and address? Or will you participate as a vendor or client of another site already established?

_____

_____

_____

_____

Confidence, comfort, and familiarity are important if you want to navigate the skies of e-commerce successfully. Depending on your age and level of experience, you may feel insecure about how to utilize available technology in pursuit of building and launching your vision online. You may need to ask for help from others, often those younger than you, and maintain a spirit of humility as an eager student.

Or you may have grown up with technology, and as a result shopping via e-commerce is more familiar than going to the mall. You have no trouble navigating and even building sites online but you struggle with the more impersonal aspects of online communication and commerce. You long for interactions just like your products or services—authentic, natural, handcrafted.

The good news is that no matter what your attitude may be toward technology and e-commerce you can still learn from others. Often pairing with someone who tilts in the opposite direction than you with regards to technology can provide both of you with a rich learning opportunity. Ideally, you learn from one another and fulfill entrepreneurial needs that you both have.

9)   On a scale of 1 to 10, with 1 being totally intimidated and 10 being fully confident, how would you rate your comfort level with the technology required to fulfill your new venture's potential?

_____

_____

_____

_____

_____

_____

10) If your confidence runs high, what are some additional ways you can maximize your expertise with technology to build and launch your vision? Which individuals, companies, stores, and organizations use technology the way you hope to use it?

_____

_____

_____

_____

_____

11) If you're feeling insecure or intimidated by technology, who are the qualified people in your network who would likely be willing to tutor you? Don't overlook your grandkids, teens in your neighborhood, and college students and other young adults at church. List the names of at least two people you know to whom you can reach out to this week for advice and assistance as you enhance your online skills.

_____

_____

_____

_____

The Golden Rule that's in the Bible, one you may recall from church, still provides wise counsel for how you relate to your customer and the shopping experience you want to provide to them. Jesus said, "Do to others what you would have them do to you" (Matt. 7:12, NIV) and exhorts us to put ourselves in someone else's shoes. I'm convinced this compassionate, respectful way of treating others holds up in all relationships, including those with your prospective customers.

12) With your new venture in mind, how can you apply the Golden Rule to your online constituents?

_____

_____

_____

_____

_____

13) What kind of experience do you want your customers, fans, followers, or participants to have as they interact with you over the internet? Brainstorm for a few moments and come up with three key adjectives to describe the experience you want to have with others online. For example, you might choose descriptors such as convenient, personal, no-frills, appealing, accessible, or easy-to-use.

Being a good online sleuth is crucial to becoming a great entrepreneur. It's not just researching information and ideas that improves your odds of getting your new venture off the ground and sustaining flight. It's how you integrate and assimilate the knowledge gleaned from your research and how you use it to influence your own designs, especially those related to your online e-commerce, that make the difference. Surfing online and taking note of sites and online retailers with features you want to emulate allows you a head start as you venture into the many exciting opportunities e-commerce provides.

14) Spend twenty minutes surfing the web, concentrating on sites that include e-commerce as a central focus. Based on your time browsing, as well as past experiences with various online merchants, what do your favorite sites tend to have in common?

_____

_____

_____

_____

_____

15) Which sites or online stores frustrate you? Why? What in particular bothers you about these sites? How can you make sure you avoid these pet peeves when launching your venture online?

_____

_____

_____

_____

_____

CHAPTER 7

⬦

Flight Crew

Assembling Your Dream Team

Building a vision and getting it off the ground often begin as a solo act for entrepreneurs. In fact, that's part of the appeal—having autonomy, freedom, and flexibility to do things your own way instead of someone else's. While relying on your own abilities, talents, and skills is crucial to your success, at some point—and I recommend sooner rather than later—you must consider building a team to support your endeavor, sustain it, and grow it. No matter how gifted or well-resourced you may be, you're still only one person, which means you're limited.

If you're going to soar, you will need to assemble a flight crew for your journey. An entrepreneurial mind-set always includes a collaborative, team approach. If you want to be truly successful over the long haul, then you must assemble the best team possible to support, sustain, and soar with your new venture.

1)   Do you consider yourself more of an independent worker or more of a team player? Why?

_____

_____

_____

_____

_____

_____

2)   What has been your past experience working as part of a larger team, department, division, committee, ministry, or other collaborative endeavor? What did you enjoy most about these experiences? And what would you want to change or avoid as you work with other teams in the future?

_____

_____

_____

_____

_____

_____

The Bible has much to say about the value of working collaboratively, especially Proverbs, a timeless collection of wisdom on virtually all subjects. There we're told, "For lack of guidance a nation falls, but victory is won through many advisers" (Prov.

11:14, NIV. For our purposes, we can replace the word *nation* with *enterprise* to reinforce the vital importance of having a vision that includes multiplying your opportunities for success by building a team.

Proverbs also warns us not to rely too much on others, particularly in loading our team with friends whose feelings, both theirs and ours, can get in the way of the business. We're told, "Many will say they are loyal friends, but who can find one who is truly reliable?" (Prov. 20:6, NLT). In fact, hiring friends will often kill your business faster than a lightning strike hitting your plane's engine. When you hire a friend, it becomes harder to push this person to their best performance. While you might think it's easier because of the rapport you have already established with a friend, most people find that their emotions get in the way.

You want your friends to keep on being your friends, and so ultimately you struggle to be honest and forthright and speak the truth in love to the friends on your team. Basically, you allow the friendship to get in the way of the entrepreneurship. Consequently, you let things slide at work because you don't want to risk hurting their feelings or stepping on their toes. You don't hold them accountable to the same standard as a team member who's not a friend, and as a result your venture suffers.

3)   Do you agree that it's generally not a good idea to hire friends for your business? What problems have you experienced working with or supervising friends in the past?

_____

_____

_____

_____

_____

_____

4) Play devil's advocate for a moment and list some advantages of hiring a friend to be part of the team for your new venture. Are these advantages worth the risk of putting the friendship before your vision—or of potentially losing a friend? Why or why not?

_____

_____

_____

_____

_____

_____

Most entrepreneurs find it's better for everyone if you separate your personal relationships from your professional ones. You want to give your new venture the time, attention, and quality of support it deserves in order to have every chance at succeeding. You're hiring others for their abilities, talents, and the contribution they can make to your venture—not for their ability to agree with you, laugh at your jokes, or catch up on mutual friends and family members.

If your team members end up being friends without it affecting their performance or yours, then enjoy this extraordinary blessing. Most of the time, however, your new venture will benefit and grow more quickly if you keep expectations clear and boundaries firmly in place. Enlist the best people to fill the roles you need filled and to do the jobs you need done as effectively as possible. Perform your due diligence into their education, training, and past experiences to increase the likelihood they will be able to share your vision for building an enterprise that can soar.

5) Think back on your past job experiences. Which coworkers did you most enjoy working with? Why? And which ones caused you to struggle in performing your responsibilities?

_____

_____

_____

_____

_____

6)   What do these past experiences with various types of coworkers tell you about the kind of people you hope to hire for your team?

_____

_____

_____

_____

_____

Emotional intelligence is usually considered a person's ability to discern and identify their own emotions as well as the feelings of others, along with their ability to use this awareness appropriately in their social context and the advancement of their goals. From my experience, emotional intelligence is a vital component, along with objective and sensory data about the situation or person under consideration, for making your best instinctive decisions. Whether you call it a "gut feeling," your intuition, or personal instinct, we all have impressions about other people that go beyond their résumés.

7) On a scale of 1 to 10, with 1 being "mostly unaware" and 10 being "usually aware," how would you rank the your awareness of your own feelings and the feelings of those around you? Give a recent example of an interaction with someone that supports the answer you chose.

_____

_____

_____

_____

_____

8) Do you tend to be overly sensitive and aware of every little nuance in a conversation? Or do you sometimes miss the vibe or undercurrent of emotion behind what was said?

_____

_____

_____

_____

_____

9) How often do you rely on first impressions and gut feelings when meeting someone for the first time? Do these tend to be accurate and hold up over time as you get to know someone? In other words, how much do you trust your feelings when interacting with someone new?

_____

_____

_____

_____

_____

_____

Ideally, every new entrepreneur would enjoy the benefit of three different kinds of ground crew members: supporters, advisers, and mentors. These relationships are not essential to your endeavor's success, but they usually lay the groundwork for the smooth runway you need in order to take flight. While these roles may overlap, let's consider each of these encouragers and the unique contribution they make to your overall achievement.

Supporters tend to be the people you consider your greatest fans, the ones who celebrate your triumphs with you as well as pick up the pieces when you fall. For many entrepreneurs, their families provide this kind of support and personal care. They not only encourage your endeavors and serve as a sounding board, they also provide practical support in the form of picking up your kids from school, cooking a meal from time to time, or offering to help out with household chores.

Advisers, on the other hand, give you professional, intellectual support, usually in the form of their counsel and wisdom. They may care about you personally but have more to offer you in the form of their best business practices. They are often entrepreneurs themselves and have already experienced many of the initial challenges you are facing. They want to help you avoid the same mistakes they made and thereby make your business more successful.

Mentors combine both of these roles, the supporter and the adviser, and offer comprehensive insight into how to juggle your life's demands as an entrepreneur with those of being a spouse, parent, caregiver, or student. They want you to succeed professionally but not at the expense of your personal life and family coherence. They know that to truly succeed you must never lose sight of life balance and the priority of loving those most important in your life.

10) Of these three types of team members, which ones are already in place? Which do you need more of to build your vision and launch it effectively?

_____

_____

_____

_____

_____

11) List the names of at least two people you know who can fill these vital roles on your team. If you haven't already discussed your new venture and what you need from them along the way, then contact them this week and schedule time together.

Supporters

_____

_____

Advisers

_____

_____

Mentors

Clear communication between you and your team members is vital for the health and growth of your new venture. Contracts, while not conducive for warm feelings, nonetheless provide a basis for establishing and understanding each other's expectations and responsibilities. They provide an objective, mutually agreeable document that outlines each other's roles, and they also establish the method by which any major conflicts will be resolved.

Make sure you have contracts with any and all investors in your venture, even if they are family (especially if they are family!) or close friends. While it's tempting to believe your relationship is strong enough to handle anything that might go wrong, you would be surprised how different people can be when tempers flare and conflicts arise. Planning and discussing in advance can make a huge difference, for the good of your new venture as well as the relationships involved.

12) How does having your business plan completed improve communications between you and prospective employees?

13) In past business dealings, have you tended to "play by the rules" most of the time (signing contracts, organizing information, maintaining clear and frequent communication, etc.), or do you like to improvise and go with what seems best for each specific project situation (agreeing with a handshake, focusing more on creative aspects than administrative ones, communicating only as needed, etc.)?

_____

_____

_____

_____

_____

14) Why is knowing yourself, both your strengths and weaknesses, crucial to hiring the best people for your new venture?

_____

_____

_____

_____

_____

CHAPTER 8

✦

What Goes Up
Must Come Down

Entrepreneurial Leadership 101

Can you imagine a pilot who knows how to take off in her plane but doesn't know how to land that metal bird? Of course not! Similarly, you begin with the end in mind and set a vision for how you want your new venture to reach its destination and fulfill your vision successfully. Your ability to see the big picture and control the process as much as possible is fundamental to being an entrepreneurial leader. It's what separates the ultrasuccessful from those who simply reach a certain altitude and coast on autopilot.

No matter how successful your venture becomes, it's not enough just to get it off the ground and in the air—you must determine where, when, and how you want to set it down. Even as it evolves and changes along the way, which it inevitably will, you still need to know what to do with what you have created. Otherwise, you're doomed to free float indefinitely, cruising at a pleasant altitude but with no destination where you can land.

1)   Have you ever started using something, perhaps an appliance or new app on your phone, without knowing how to operate it fully? What's usually the result?

_____

_____

_____

_____

2)   Have you already considered where you want to take your new venture and envisioned a future endpoint? What currently motivates the result you would want to achieve as you bring your vision to life?

_____

_____

_____

_____

Thinking through the conclusion of this epic vision you're building may seem impossible at this point because so many variables of your success are yet to be determined. And while it's true you will encounter many ups and downs that must be evaluated and integrated throughout your flight, you nonetheless must do everything in your power to prepare for the future landing you hope to secure.

Consider all possibilities for where you want to take this vision you're building. Is this new venture one you hope to pass on to your children and grandchildren or to sell and liquidate down the road? Are you hoping to be bought out by a large conglomerate competitor or dreaming of taking your private venture public by selling shares to global investors? Are you motivated to launch this side-hustle to supplement your retirement income or wanting something to engage your imagination and exercise the years of experience you had working for someone else? Do you want a passive partnership in exchange for a guaranteed retirement income or would you rather have a lump sum right now? Knowing how you want to land your plane is just as important before takeoff as after you're in the air.

3)   Which of the following would you include as part of your new venture's final destination? Check all that apply.
- ☐ A short-term (1–3 years) money-making venture
- ☐ A long-term (5–20+ years) investment to be liquidated or sold
- ☐ A part-time venture to supplement your current career
- ☐ A passionate pursuit in which to become expert
- ☐ A hobby to occupy your free time
- ☐ A legacy for your family to inherit and continue to build on
- ☐ A legacy for your family to sell or cash out
- ☐ A solution to a social problem
- ☐ A ministry to help a specific group or to address a certain issue or social problem
- ☐ Something else: (write it here) _____

4)   Obviously, no one can predict the future with 100 percent accuracy, but what prevents or inhibits you from envisioning where you would like your new venture to end up? How can you overcome these barriers so as to see more clearly where you would like to go?

_____

_____

_____

_____

Understanding what you hope, envision, want, and would like to happen is crucial to how you build your vision from the ground up. With a sense of your ideal future landing strip in mind, you can then make so many other choices with much more accuracy, efficiency, and intentionality. In fact, beginning with the end in mind will make many of your daily decisions for you.

For example, consider the way many investors buy a property knowing they intend to flip it—to renovate, remodel, and redesign it before reselling it for a profit. These flippers usually ignore their own personal tastes and style preferences in favor of more generic, neutral colors and décor. They want their renovated property to appeal to the broadest consumer market possible.

Real estate flippers also choose cheaper materials to keep costs down. Sometimes they can even buy fixtures, finishes, and furniture for a lower cost in bulk to use for several properties and not just one. Because they know their goal and their time line, they don't spend over budget on expensive, distinct design elements that would only appeal to a handful of buyers. They begin with the end in mind, planning to land in a way that will allow them to exit with the maximum profit for their investment.

5) If you knew exactly where your new business or venture would be in five years, how would this knowledge affect the decisions you're making right now about how to get it off the ground?

_____

_____

_____

_____

_____

6) In two or three sentences, describe where and how you would like to see your venture conclude, assuming a best-case scenario. Be as specific as possible!

———————————————————————————————

———————————————————————————————

———————————————————————————————

———————————————————————————————

Thinking through all aspects of your new venture's flight pattern from takeoff to landing provides numerous benefits. These include anticipating potential problems before they develop and establishing procedural solutions should they arise. With the many vendors and subcontractors my companies sometimes use, I make sure that we include a clear arbitration clause in case something goes off track. We include these rules of disengagement while everyone is friendly and enthused about our collaboration because we know that it can become very challenging to communicate when things turn sour.

Many couples sign prenuptial agreements for the same reason—*before* they walk down the aisle and join their lives together legally, financially, and emotionally. As awkward and uncomfortable as it might feel, it's easier to come up with practical rules of dissolving their union while they're lovingly devoted to each other rather than waiting until something happens to burst the bubble of their marital bliss. They know that thinking through the future's worst-case scenarios affords them the freedom to commit to each other wholeheartedly in the present.

7)   Do you agree that your venture will be stronger if you plan ahead for how you will handle conflict and address problems? Why or why not?

———————————————————————————————

———————————————————————————————

———————————————————————————————

———————————————————————————————

8) Assuming you agree that there's wisdom in proactively diverting drama when you face future challenges, what action do you need to take in building your vision right now?

_____

_____

_____

_____

Thinking through where you want your new venture to land, how would you want to leave the business in an ideal situation? This process can often be more complicated than you realize here at the beginning. For instance, if your name is on the business or closely associated with it, are you willing to allow your name to be used after you sell it? What about your image? Many successful ventures sell their name or buy the rights to partner with another company so that their names and brands become associated.

9) Assuming your venture matures successfully, how would you ideally like to exit? If you sold it, would you want to work for your buyer? Would you want to start another new, similar venture? Leave it and stop working entirely?

_____

_____

_____

_____

10) Describe your ideal role after bringing your successful venture to a close. Be as detailed as possible about what you would and would not be willing to continue doing or contributing.

_____

_____

_____

_____

Once you've built and launched your new venture, it will likely travel at a speed that's all its own, a pace you will likely discover once you're off the ground. It may not be as fast as you would like, but nonetheless it may be a pace faster than you can comfortably keep up with. You might think you want instant success so that you can continue investing and growing your venture into something larger and even more successful.

But the reality is that this kind of extraordinary growth requires ordinary, daily dedicated effort and incredible patience. You'll likely experience seasons when your venture's growth is slow and steady. Other times, you will feel like you're in a holding pattern and just maintaining status quo. And if you're blessed with a tailwind in the form of phenomenal opportunities, you will also encounter dramatic times of unexpected acceleration. You must be mentally prepared and physically equipped to endure all speeds.

11) In an ideal situation, how many hours per week would you want to spend working on your new venture? Is this reasonable considering all the attention and energy your endeavor will require to succeed at the level of your ultimate vision?

_____

_____

_____

_____

_____

12) Knowing your other commitments and responsibilities, how can you learn to adjust to the variable speed of your venture's growth? What steps can you take now that will make it easier for you to adjust as the need arises?

_____

_____

_____

_____

_____

CHAPTER 9

⊷◇⊶

Fail Fast and Crash Last

Entrepreneurial Leadership 102

Every entrepreneur, inventor, innovator, and artist inevitably encounters obstacles, challenges, and detours in the path of their creation's trajectory. The successful ones learn the art of improvisation that's backed up by the information of scientific study and the skill set of their life's experiences. They expect to face highs and lows that they simply cannot imagine at the beginning when they are building their vision and getting it off the ground.

You can learn much about the power of improvisation just by remaining self-aware and engaged with what's going on around you. I'm convinced improvisation is a skill we must all practice and hone long before anything goes wrong. This skill requires preparation, engagement, resourcefulness, and creativity to come up with solutions when your new venture faces the unexpected. The best entrepreneurial thinkers, like the heroic "Sully" Sullenberger, can land gracefully even in the most turbulent circumstances.

1) Do you remember what you first thought and felt when you heard about the "Miracle on the Hudson," US Airways Flight 1549's dramatic emergency landing on the Hudson River in 2009?

_____

_____

_____

_____

_____

_____

2)   Have you ever been through an unexpected crisis situation where you had to make quick decisions that carried huge consequences? Did you take immediate action and know what to do? Or did you hesitate and try to stall for time? What have you learned about yourself from these situations?

_____

_____

_____

_____

_____

Many entrepreneurs struggle the most with their own expectations, their own impatience and unfamiliarity with the stop-and-start, hurry-up-and-wait, trial-and-error nature of the process involved in starting a new venture. While you can do your best to create checklists, ideal time lines, and organizational charts, the reality when you're launching your venture will often require you to "wing it until you can bring it!" Basically, you must have clear targets, goals, and systems while remaining flexible enough to adapt to the realities of operation as you discover them.

3) How do you typically function under pressure? Do you tend to thrive when you're forced into a corner or to shut down and become paralyzed?

_____

_____

_____

_____

4) Do you prefer to have organized structure and clear definition when tackling a project or to improvise and make up the rules as you go along?

_____

_____

_____

_____

5) Reflecting on your past work experience, would others with whom you worked describe you as a flexible worker? Would you agree with their assessment? Why or why not?

_____

_____

_____

_____

My friend Oprah Winfrey once described failure as nothing more than a stepping-stone to future success. I love her perspective! You see, a stepping-stone merely provides a means to an end. It's basically just a mile marker between where you are and where you're going—it's never your ultimate destination. Can you imagine driving along a highway and then parking in the middle of a bridge? No—the bridge is there to help you get from one place to another!

Providing a temporary foothold or handle, bridges and stepping-stones link one experience to another, allowing you to move forward, even if it's a smaller step than you hoped. Stepping-stones are often lateral moves and don't move you forward at all—they may even require you to step back and regroup before you leap forward again. But all of them provide you with a place to move next, a spot to take in the view, catch your breath, and get a new perspective. One day's failure may actually be tomorrow's bridge to success!

6) Describe your attitude toward failing. Do you tend to criticize yourself and lose confidence when things don't go as planned? Or are you more likely to deflect responsibility and blame other factors?

_____

_____

_____

_____

_____

7) For you personally, why is it so important to separate your feelings about failure from your actions?

_____

_____

_____

_____

_____

_____

8)   How do you usually blow off steam and handle stress in your life? Will this method work once the pressure increases as you're building your vision? What else can you do to maintain perspective and reduce the natural stress that's bound to occur?

_____

_____

_____

_____

_____

Everyone fails and makes choices they later regret. I suspect those who grow the most aren't the people who never fail but the ones who learn from their fall and get back up again and keep going. This is what I see with two of Jesus's disciples who both failed him in one of his hours of greatest need. Judas betrayed Christ for thirty pieces of silver and handed his master over to the authorities (Luke 22:1–38). After Jesus was arrested that same night, Peter denied even knowing Jesus—not once but three times (Luke 22:54–63).

Each disciple handled his failure in dramatically different ways, however. Judas apparently could not live with his guilt and shame over betraying Jesus and ended up taking his own life. Peter, on the other hand, accepted the Lord's forgiveness and went on to become foundational for the Christian church. One couldn't get past what he had done and the other learned to put it in his past.

9) Can you relate more to Judas or to Peter? Do you tend to brood on your past mistakes or are you usually able to shake them off and move forward?

_____

_____

_____

_____

_____

10) How will your natural tendencies to handle mistakes affect the launch of your vision? In what ways can you use your faith and the power of grace and forgiveness to assist you in learning from mistakes?

_____

_____

_____

_____

_____

As we've discussed, most bridges are designed and constructed of flexible materials that allow them to expand and contract based on weather conditions and temperatures. Entrepreneurial thinkers do the same thing as they're constructing their vision. They are optimistic realists who hope for the best but prepare for the worst. They expect to succeed but aren't discouraged when challenges present themselves.

Ironically, many new entrepreneurs seem to suffer most from being successful too early in their ascent. They prepared for almost every scenario—except quick success!

Remember, a blessing too fast is no blessing at all! You have to know your capacity, and that means identifying your limitations and liabilities. Savvy awareness also entails knowing exactly who your ideal customer is and everything about them. Such knowledge will help you anticipate product demand and sales cycles, which in turn can influence the way you manage inventory and handle marketing.

11) How much growth can your present design accommodate in the first year of launching your vision?

_____

_____

_____

_____

_____

12) What's required for it to double in size within your first year? Triple? How can you provide more room to grow in the design of your vision before you build it?

_____

_____

_____

_____

Whether you like it or not, your age and stage of life directly influence your vision and the way you go about constructing it. Generational dynamics have an impact on your design, development, and execution throughout the process. From your knowledge and experience of popular culture to your attitudes toward social issues to your understanding of technology, you must own generational assets as well as acknowledge your limitations. You must also understand the generational gap between you and your target constituents.

Closing these gaps and connecting across generations and demographic differences is vital for the success of your venture. When you can see your products and services the way others view them, you can make your offerings more appealing, more relevant, and more enticing to your target consumers. Or, if you choose to ignore such blind spots, you will likely limit your constituency to only people exactly like you.

13) Do you consider yourself a baby boomer (usually born after World War II and before 1965), a member of Generation X (from the early 1960s to 1980s), or a millennial (born after 1990)? How would you describe your own generation?

_____

_____

_____

_____

_____

14) What are the key differences between your own age and generation and the ages and generational attitudes of your target customers or constituents? How do these differences affect the way you're building and launching your vision?

_____

_____

_____

_____

_____

15) Contact at least one person you know well from a generation older than your own as well as someone from a generation younger than your own. Ask each of them to provide feedback on your mission statement and overall business plan.

_____

_____

_____

_____

_____

CHAPTER 10

✦

Growing Forward

Minding Your Own Business

Have you ever felt constrained by the perceptions and expectations of others? That was my experience as my ministry grew and I became more successful in my various entrepreneurial endeavors. As I share in this chapter, I knew it was time for a change, a big move to a location where I could realize the full potential indicated by my various growing pains. While some people around me couldn't understand my impetus, I refused to be limited by their lack of imagination and vision for my future. I knew my journey would be unique and did what was necessary to have all I would need to grow at full capacity.

If you can relate to this feeling of being misunderstood as you build and launch your vision, then your path requires full confidence in yourself and your ability to bring your dreams to life. My vision had outgrown its environment, and a change was required to take me from my homeland to my divinely appointed destination. Throughout the process, I learned that my ultimate purpose provided a powerful north star to my entrepreneurial inner compass.

1) When have you experienced personal growing pains in your career or professional endeavors?

_____

_____

_____

_____

_____

2)   Do you often settle for status quo and keep things at their current level or are you more likely to shake things up as you strive for more?

_____

_____

_____

_____

3)   How have others' perceptions of you influenced your decisions as you attempt to fulfill your purpose?

_____

_____

_____

_____

Purpose, power, and profit each plays a role in accomplishing what I like to call impact. When you consider impact, you're basically determining the level of results your efforts have on your department, company, community, city, and society. If impact is a quantifiable method of evaluating relevance, one cannot measure accomplishment without getting immersed in the metrics of success. Just as a short-distance runner needs a stopwatch to determine his ability to meet his goal in the 400-yard dash, one must be prepared to consider the specific metrics used to determine success.

You see, business success isn't measured by longevity alone. The fact that the business is sustained over a particular time period doesn't necessarily mean that it's profitable. Nonprofits cannot be measured by adherence to purpose alone because in order to remain functional they must remain profitable on many levels. Their impact must be determined by a comparison of quantifiable metrics: How many people did we feed? How much did it cost us? How long can we operate this way? How does this fit with our projected budget for this month, this quarter, this year? Such questions require metrics to provide answers on an organization's impact.

Often, considering something or someone successful becomes a matter of subjective opinion rather than quantifiable growth. But most of us have specific criteria we use, even if we're not consciously aware of it, to define success. While profit on a quarterly and annual basis is one way to measure your new venture's success, I recommend you also consider its impact—the time and energy required to produce this amount of profit.

4) What criteria do you typically use when deeming something or someone successful? For example, if they make a certain amount of money, handle a certain number of customers, or exhibit certain physical status symbols, such as a large office.

_____

_____

_____

_____

_____

5)   More importantly, what criteria will you use to measure the growth and success of your new venture?

_____

_____

_____

_____

_____

A successful entrepreneur worth several hundred million dollars recently told me he works an average of 95 to 100 hours a week. After starting a successful software business out of college, he sold it ten years later for millions of dollars. Since then, he has concentrated on utilizing technology in real estate and construction investments. Many would describe him as a workaholic with little time to actually enjoy life. Others would consider him a role model and the pinnacle of entrepreneurial success.

6)   What would you consider him in light of knowing what it will cost you for your venture to succeed? How much is your personal time and energy worth? In other words, how much of yourself are you willing to invest in your venture in return for what it produces?

_____

_____

_____

_____

7) Do you agree that measuring your endeavor's impact is an important way to gauge its ultimate success?

_____

_____

_____

_____

_____

8) What impact do you want your new venture to have—on your own life? On your customers' or constituents' lives? On the community you serve?

_____

_____

_____

_____

_____

An entrepreneurial mind-set is all about considering the variables required to produce certain outcomes. Over the years, I have come to look at both my return on investment (ROI) and my effort to impact (E2I) ratio when evaluating most major decisions. I ask myself, "Considering all that I will invest into this direction, will the return be commensurate with the energy I expend? Or should I put my efforts elsewhere and reconsider the value of my time and my energy for what will be returned?"

9) I once heard someone say, "Anyone can be rich if they're willing to pay the price." What do you think they meant by this statement? Do you agree with them? Why or why not?

_____

_____

_____

_____

_____

10) How would you currently describe or calculate your E2I for building and launching your vision? In other words, do you believe what you're doing will consequently produce more than you're investing with your time, energy, and effort?

_____

_____

_____

_____

_____

When you first launch your new venture, it often feels like you're spinning your wheels. No matter how much effort you expend, you don't seem to see any impact, whether on your business, your nonprofit, your ministry, or whatever you're launching. From my experience, you can usually correct the problem by no longer expending your greatest effort in the wrong places. Misplaced priorities can cause your E2I ratio to be as powerless as an impotent swing during a bad dream. Instead, aim your efforts at the places within your target where you can have the greatest impact. This contact point insures the greatest impact for the expenditure of your energy and effort.

11) Think of a time recently when you've been frustrated by getting little return on a large investment of your time and energy? What were you hoping to get in return? What did you actually receive?

_____

_____

_____

_____

_____

_____

12) Are you aiming your current efforts into the right areas in order to build and launch your vision successfully?

Complete the following statements:

The most important thing I must do next to build my vision is _____

_____.

I need to stop pouring so much time and effort into _____
_____ **because it's not producing
the kind of results I want as I move forward with building my vision.**

I fear many people are happy to live their lives based on the superficial appearance of success versus the actuality of a life fulfilled. As long as they appear successful, they don't have to consider that the engine of their enterprise may not be effectively taking them to the destination of real success. While the outside of their venture sparkles and gleams, it can't sustain flight for the long haul that is required to carry them to their highest potential.

This contrast illustrates the problem with operating your life without looking at the metrics: of the many initiatives you're pursuing, you can't effectively evaluate which are working *for* you and which are working *on* you. Is your energy having impact or is it merely expended without a significant return? *Impact determines success.* How else will you feel accomplished if your only measurement is survival-based or reliant only on appearances? You want ultimate success, not just a temporary veneer!

13) How concerned are you about *appearing* successful with your new venture as opposed to actually having the impact you want to have and being successful?

_____

_____

_____

_____

_____

_____

_____

14) How much time, energy, and effort are you presently expending in an attempt to look successful at this point in your life? Is this effective in accomplishing your dream and launching your vision? Or is it potentially distracting you and holding you back?

_____

_____

_____

_____

15) Do you agree that impact ultimately determines success? Why or why not?

_____

_____

_____

_____

16) What steps do you need to take next to increase your emphasis on impact? Check all that apply.

- ☐ Talk to an attorney concerning my questions
- ☐ Talk to an accountant about taxes, payroll, pensions, and/or other financial matters
- ☐ Talk to a tech expert about my website, social media, and related matters
- ☐ Talk to potential subcontractors needed to build or launch my vision
- ☐ Revise my profit margins for the first years of my business
- ☐ Draft a community development plan for my venture

☐ Draft an evaluation form for all clients, customers, and constituents to use

☐ Other impact-related steps: (write them here)

_____

_____

_____

_____

CHAPTER 11

❖

The Miracle of Marketing

Burning Your Bushel to Fly Higher

It might have been tempting to settle for flying planes from continent to continent, but entrepreneurial visionaries have kept pushing the boundaries of known science as they reach for new heights of success. Today, those once fixed boundaries of flight continue to be stretched and extended as commercial space flights are becoming reality. Private companies such as Virgin Galactic, SpaceX, and Blue Origin have been pursuing commercial human spaceflight for the past two decades.

As I'm writing this, they, along with several other corporate ventures, continue to develop programs that would transport public passengers into the cosmos (http://www.space.com/24249-commercial-space-travel-blasts-off-2014.html). Who knows? In your lifetime, you may be able to take a space shuttle to the moon, to Mars, or beyond! The fact remains that an entrepreneurial mind-set never rests on its past accomplishments and is always pushing for progress.

1)   Which technological advancements or cultural changes in your lifetime have surprised you the most? Which ones have paved the way to allow you to build and launch your vision more effectively and efficiently?

_____

_____

_____

_____

_____

2) Who are the entrepreneurial pioneers who, much like the ladies in *Hidden Figures*, transcended the confines culture placed on them in the field or area in which you're bringing your dream to life? Which ones have influenced and inspired you the most? Why?

_____

_____

_____

_____

_____

Effective marketing is essential to the ultimate success of your business. While you may understand its impact on launching your business, many new entrepreneurs underestimate the vital role marketing plays in sustaining flight and reaching their destination. From my experience, marketing effectively is an ongoing educational process and requires keen attention to cultural trends, exact timing, and customer relations. You have to know who you are as well as who your customer is—even as both are constantly changing!

I've been told by many small-business owners that they consider marketing a burdensome, necessary chore to keep their business running, much like filling out tax forms or taking the trash out. When I encounter people with this attitude toward marketing, I try to inspire them to be more creative, more original, more personal in their ongoing marketing efforts. I'm convinced the best marketing is organic and integrated into who you are, what you're selling, why you're selling it, and who you're trying to reach. The best marketing efforts gradually become synonymous with your brand even as they extend, enhance, and enforce that brand.

3)   Do you agree that marketing is vital to the success of your new venture? Which marketing channels do you consider the most important to reach your target audience? Why?

_____

_____

_____

_____

4)   Do you consider yourself more of a natural marketer, outgoing and extroverted, or do you feel more introverted and reserved, struggling to promote yourself and your endeavors? What impact will your natural marketing tendencies have on the construction and launch of your vision?

_____

_____

_____

———————————————————————————————

———————————————————————————————

———————————————————————————————

As I share in this chapter, I never intended to brand myself specifically as an entrepreneur, but over the years I discovered its umbrella covers my many ministry interests and creative ventures quite well. It provides me with flexibility to initiate many diverse endeavors while keeping them all true to my unique calling and gifting. Consequently, I would caution you against being too narrow with your brand identity and marketing efforts, because you want to leave room for growth and expansion—possibly in areas that may not occur to you when starting out. Instead, find a way to incorporate your mission into your marketing.

This is the process that has worked for me. You see, early on I realized that everything I do—from ministry to music to movies and beyond—revolves around my desire to inform, inspire, and entertain people. I believe lives can be changed and transformed through those three relational pillars, so I have built my ministry, my conferences, my books—everything I do—around making sure they all reflect enlightening information, innovative inspiration, and exceptional entertainment. My faith unites them all just as my body contains all the parts, both visible and invisible, of who I am.

5) Review the list of marketing channels and methods below and consider the role each one will likely play in the successful launch and flight of your endeavor. Now rank them, with 1 being the most important and 10 being the least important, to help you prioritize these pieces for your overall marketing strategy.
- ☐ Print media such as flyers, postcards, bulletin board announcements, etc.
- ☐ Dedicated website with monthly updates
- ☐ Twitter account with at least weekly tweets
- ☐ Facebook page with customer "likes"
- ☐ Radio commercials on local channels within your community
- ☐ Television commercials within your state or multistate region
- ☐ Community sponsorship of local sports teams, schools, and churches

- ☐ Banner ads and pop-up ads on selected websites
- ☐ Email blasts to a list of customers, supporters, and subscribers
- ☐ Promotional products such as T-shirts, key chains, and magnets

I find it so remarkable that Jesus preached one of his longest messages to 5,000 men (not to mention their wives, children, and other family members), but not one word in the Bible tells us what he actually said! Instead, what we find in Scripture (Matt. 14:18–24) focused on what he *did* for his audience after he finished teaching.

After polling the people to see what food he could work with, Jesus took the five loaves and two fish a little boy had brought for lunch, and looking up to heaven, Christ gave thanks and broke the bread. Then he handed the food over to his disciples, who in turn distributed these most unique fish sandwiches to the thousands of people present that day. We're told everyone ate until they were full, and then the disciples picked up twelve baskets of leftovers. This may have been the first church potluck on record!

6) Imagine you were one of the people present at that glorious picnic with Jesus, sitting with your family eating bread and fish that the disciples distributed. Assuming you had never heard of Jesus prior to this miraculous event, what would you tell others about your experience the next day? What would you tell them about Jesus?

_____

_____

_____

_____

_____

7) Have you ever considered that *how* you relate to your constituents is just as important as your actual product, service, ministry, or cause? What are some unique or

creative ways you can reach, connect, and impress your potential donors, customers, and clients?

_____

_____

_____

_____

_____

8) Brainstorm at least three unconventional methods below. Include all possibilities, even those that may seem too expensive, crazy, or over-the-top!

_____

_____

_____

_____

_____

In a statement that illuminates fittingly enough what he had done by feeding the 5,000, Jesus later explained, "Neither do men light a candle and hide it under a bushel" (Matt. 5:15, NIV). I'm fairly certain he was referring to the way human beings naturally want to share the news when good things happen. While Jesus was emphasizing the way his followers reflected the light of God, I believe this observation holds true for us as entrepreneurs as well. If we have something we truly believe in, then we mustn't keep it a secret!

Unfortunately, we often get so caught up in running the business that we overlook the importance of communicating all we have to offer. Visionaries often overlook the qualifications that uniquely equip them to bring their personal dreams to life. These qualities are part of their brand and therefore part of what they can use to market their new venture and to build rapport with their constituents. Developing an entrepreneurial mind-set means overcoming any shyness, modesty, or insecurity you hold and instead cultivating openness, directness, and confidence as you communicate with others.

9) After reflecting for a few moments, list all personal talents, abilities, experiences, and achievements that will assist you in marketing your new venture. For example, perhaps you have a degree in communications, job experience in human resources, volunteer experience with children, and a background in musical performance. Can you see how these would be great assets for someone launching a new community youth center? Now consider your own!

_____

_____

_____

_____

_____

10) What story do you want to tell with your new venture? What narrative style best suits this story—funny, dramatic, compassionate, silly, warm, conversational—or something else?

_____

_____

_____

_____

_____

_____

As you near the end of this process we have been exploring together, now is a good time to review what you've learned about your vision, how you want to build it, and what it will take for it to succeed over the long haul. You still have plenty of time to make changes, revise outdated data, and refresh the brand you want to convey to consumers. Utilizing your entrepreneurial attitude allows you to continually make needed changes based on your latest inspiration, investigation, and integration.

11) Answer the following questions as quickly and concisely as possible:

What is the name of your new venture?

_____

In one sentence or less, what is its primary purpose or mission?

_____

In one sentence or less, who is your specific target audience? In other words, who most needs what you're providing?

_____

What logo, mascot, slogan, jingle, font style, or other identifying tags will be part of your venture's core identity?

_____

How will these identifiers make your venture more memorable for your constituents?

_____

12) Now go back and reconsider your answers and their overall effectiveness in identifying, branding, and selling your product, service, mission, or cause. Make any changes you consider necessary. Now ask a trusted friend, mentor, or potential constituent to review and discuss your answers as well. Make any final changes required for your new venture to soar!

_____

_____

_____

_____

_____

CHAPTER 12

⋐◇⋑

New Frontiers

Creating Your Legacy

Milestones such as birthdays and anniversaries can sometimes be bittersweet as we celebrate all our blessings as well as reflect on dreams that remain unrealized. But it's never too late! If you've made it to this point in reading *SOAR!* and working through this study guide, then you are indeed serious about building your vision and succeeding with it. No matter if you're sixteen or sixty, you are uniquely equipped to bring your entrepreneurial vision to life, to grow it into a thriving success, and to leave a legacy of wisdom, wealth, and worth to those behind you.

Whether you're a millennial just starting out or a retired baby boomer wondering if you dare start a new venture at this age and stage, you have what it takes to soar, my friend! It's time to eradicate your life of old excuses once and for all and make some decisions that can change the rest of your life, decisions that can also change the impact your new venture could have for generations to come.

1) When was the last time you celebrated a major milestone or accomplishment? How did you celebrate? Describe your feelings about this event and all that it stirred inside you.

_____

_____

_____

_____

_____

2) What professional regrets do you have? What would you do differently in your career if you were starting over again? What's keeping you from moving in this direction right now?

_____

_____

_____

_____

_____

So often we develop a persona or public role that does not accurately reflect our true identity, purpose, and gifting. We succumb to the pressures exerted by circumstances seemingly beyond our control and conform to the expectations of others around us. As you begin building your vision and launching your dreams, you may discover that others are uncomfortable with your new direction. They may prefer you to remain where you are and doing what you've been doing for a long time. They may even feel threatened by the creative energy and visionary action you're now initiating at this stage of your life.

Communicating your dreams and their passionate significance to other people often goes a long way toward getting them on board with your new direction. And if they're not willing to support, or at least refrain from impeding, your progress, then you must accept the fact that they care more about who they want you to be than who you really are. Having an entrepreneurial mind-set is about coming to terms with all that you really are and expressing it through your new venture. Being authentic, exercising your strengths and accommodating your weaknesses, and offering a part of yourself and your abilities all have the power to improve the lives of others.

3)   What assumptions about yourself have limited your entrepreneurial progress in the past? Which personal assumptions and expectations are limiting the construction of your vision right now?

_____

_____

_____

_____

_____

4)   Which of your personal gifts, talents, and abilities have been underutilized in the past? How can these be included as you build and launch your vision? In other words, how can you bring all of who you are to this exciting new venture?

_____

_____

_____

_____

_____

5) Websites for corporate, nonprofit, and ministry organizations often include a section labeled "About Us" that describes the founding and development of the enterprise. Imagining where you want your new venture to be in three years, draft an "About Us" description for your venture.

_____

_____

_____

_____

6) These "About Us" sections also often include a professional biography of the key people in the organization. Once again, imagining where you want your venture to be in three years, draft a professional bio for yourself that reflects your true self.

_____

_____

_____

_____

Sacrifice is part of the price of any great venture. My mother used to say, "You get what you pay for," which means that goods and services that are cheap often reflect poor quality. While this is certainly not true with all products and services, there's a core wisdom here that continues to resonate. If you want to offer something of considerable value to your constituents, then you must be willing to invest in your endeavor accordingly.

We see this truth spotlighted in the Bible as well. In his parables describing God's kingdom, Jesus said, "The kingdom of heaven is like treasure hidden in a field. When a man found it, he hid it again, and then in his joy went and sold all he had and bought that field. Again, the kingdom of heaven is like a merchant looking for fine pearls. When he found one of great value, he went away and sold everything he had and bought it" (Matt. 13:44–46, NIV). Now, your entrepreneurial endeavor is certainly not of value equal to the kingdom of heaven, but if your venture reflects the dream God has placed in your heart, then it is worth sacrificing for nonetheless. Many times in order for the reward to be greater the investment must be greater as well.

7) What sacrifices have you made to get to this point in your life professionally? Which sacrifices have you refused to make for your work in the past?

_____

_____

_____

_____

8) What sacrifices will you have to make to successfully build and launch your vision? In other words, what price are you willing to pay to bring your dream to life?

_____

_____

_____

_____

In the Book of Hebrews, we find a Who's Who of the Bible that recounts what many of the faithful elite faced, overcame, and became remembered for. To set up this catalog of faith-fueled heroes, this passage begins by defining faith as "the substance of things hoped for and the evidence of things not seen" (Heb. 11:1, NIV). These two ingredients, *substance* of what you hoped for and *evidence* of what was once only a dream, provide a divine recipe for faith that extends beyond our religion, denomination, or place of worship. Your faith extends as well to building and launching this God-breathed dream that you've been carrying around inside you.

Without a strong foundation of faith, you would have given up your dreams a long time ago. But if you're still reading this, you obviously haven't give up hope! You are still pursuing this vision and willing to now take action to make it a reality. Applied to our faith in what God wants to do with our new venture, evidence emerges as we see God bless our endeavors and anoint our actions. He has brought you to this point in time for a reason—it's time to fulfill your calling, not in part but in its entirety! It's time to be all God made you to be.

9) Which stories in the Bible sustained, nourished, and inspired you the most when you were growing up? What appealed to you about these stories?

_____

_____

_____

_____

_____

10) Read all of Hebrews 11. Who are the individuals from the pages of the Bible mentioned here who speak to you the most right now as you build and launch your new venture?

_____

_____

_____

_____

_____

11) How is your faith being exercised in the construction and execution of your vision? How much have you relied on faith to get this far?

_____

_____

_____

12) How could you strengthen the faith component of this endeavor? More prayer? More fellowship with other believers? More personal time alone with God?

_____

_____

_____

_____

What are you waiting for? Time is of the essence, my friend, and although it is never too late to get started, you do not want to waste any more time dwelling on the past or loitering in the present when you could be investing in your future! Now is the time to begin the hard work required to start your new venture. Now is the time to step out in faith and ask God to bless your efforts and give you guidance and wisdom. Now is the time, to quote the iconic Nike slogan, to just do it!

I suspect you aren't even aware of how much power you have within you to succeed. There is no limit to all that you can do with what God has given you. So take flight and enjoy the view as your feet leave the ground and your dreams begin to soar! My prayers and hopes are with you, trusting in your ultimate success, as you close these pages and take a giant step forward in making your dreams a reality at last.

13) What has been the biggest surprise for you while reading this book? How has this changed the way you view the work that's ahead of you?

_____

_____

_____

_____

14) Now that you've finished both *SOAR!* and this study guide, what's the next step for you to move forward? Don't delay—do it today! Godspeed, my friend!

_____

_____

_____

_____

Notes

NOTES